WE WHO WERE RAISED POOR

ENDING THE OPPRESSION OF CLASSISM

BY GWEN BROWN

WE WHO WERE RAISED POOR
ENDING THE OPPRESSION OF CLASSISM

From talks given at Appel Farm, New Jersey, May 1991

Welcome to this workshop for "Co-Counselors who were raised poor." You are wanted here.

WHAT HAPPENED TO YOU?

How many of you—

* grew up middle-class but had at least one parent who grew up poor?

* grew up low-income working-class?

* grew up poor?

* grew up on welfare?

* grew up in the projects?

* grew up being raised by someone other than your parent?

* grew up with one parent only?

* grew up without electricity or having it turned off sometimes?

* grew up without enough heat?

* grew up having to go hungry sometimes?

* grew up with violence in your home?

* grew up with a major addiction in the house?

- grew up going short on medical care?

- grew up being homeless at one point or another?

- grew up with language or grammar that didn't match that used in the schools?

- grew up watching humiliation, timidity, shame, or rage on your parents' faces?

- grew up having to steal to "make it"?

- grew up without confident models for male and female leadership?

- were left alone unattended for long periods of time before you were seven?

- were sexually abused?

- have or have had a relative in jail?

- were in jail yourself?

- experienced teasing or fear of being left out because your clothes or manners weren't acceptable?

- were humiliated in some other way?

- had parents who had experienced school failure?

- were told or in some way got the message that you were stupid or inferior?

- were told that you were stupid or inferior because you weren't white?

- have problems around money? organization? being on time? neatness?

- have an addiction?

- struggle with overeating problems?

- struggle with feelings of timidity, insignificance, worth-lessness, anger, and hopelessness?

- just don't feel good enough to do what needs to be done?

Welcome to all of you. Already one can sense that the safety here is good. Can you feel the warmth, the encouragement, and the realness? My hope for this workshop is that it will be an important turning point for you in your own struggle to make your life all that you want it to be.

We have people here from as far west as Chicago, as far south as Florida, and as far north as Maine. Look around. We are an exciting and powerful group.

I am very pleased to be the new International Liberation Reference Person for people who were raised poor. I get to know all of you, and I get to spearhead a very important movement. I hope you will see me as both fully a leader and fully your peer, at the same time. I am excited to have this opportunity to begin discharging and thinking with all of you about our past, our present situation, our long-term goals and our next steps. What a great opportunity for closeness and for world change this workshop provides.

If I say things here that you disagree with (politically or otherwise), that's fine. I'll present things the way I see them, but we all are expected to keep thinking and learning, and *everyone* in RC is free to have his or her own position on *everything*. Don't give up on your thinking around anyone. Let's keep discharging on where we disagree. Eventually real thinking and real solutions will emerge for us all.

I'd like to see each one of you plan on getting a big piece of yourself back this weekend. This is the place; this the time; this is the group that you've been waiting for. So "client" well here. Show yourself. Show the humiliation. Show how much things matter to you. Show how much you love. Let your broken heart bleed. Go for the terror, and, most of all, for the outrage of it all. We were born with a deep sense of correctness and justice that was offended early on. The outrages of this must be discharged for us to reclaim our confidence and power.

GIVING EACH OTHER UNWAVERING RESPECT

You are in a room full of deeply good people. Each and every one is a treasure. You are in a room full of people who are smart and competent and lovable, but who have rarely been treated that way. Most people here have been used, abused, and left alone to feel inadequate and to blame themselves for failures which are in fact the failures of the larger society. We've had to fight for ourselves. Our determination got us this far, but along the way we've developed some ways to survive that are no longer useful. I will need your help here this weekend to create the kind of change we want.

People here have not gotten enough deep love and respect, and some may have patterns that tend to hook behaviors in you that are less than fully loving and respectful. Try to handle your side of the interaction. Don't let other people's unaware or irrational behaviors hook you. Notice these behaviors and remember the person has been mistreated and return their unawareness with firm respect. You don't have to allow yourself to be misused, but respectfully stop things that are "off." Stay confident of your worth and theirs.

We need to be unwavering in the deep regard, radical respect, and thoughtful challenge we hold up for ourselves and for one another. Let's just decide now not to rehearse the internalized oppression at one another.

We've all had way more than enough of it. Let us challenge one another to stand tall, and let's assume that the person sitting next to us, no matter what his or her patterns, is a potential Martin Luther King, Jr., just waiting for our respect and good attention so that he or she can discharge his or her patterns and begin leading brilliantly.

Let's make this workshop a powerful beginning to a worldwide movement of poor people, one that is different from any other in history because this time we get to discharge and reclaim more and more real intelligence as we go. Let's show our respect, too, by showing up on time for sessions and classes and by making sure that things go well around us. Let's all be in charge of this workshop. Our goal is to relearn how to be fully thoughtful of ourselves and fully thoughtful of others at the same time. That's what real power is all about.

ESTABLISHING UNITY

It is essential to our progress toward unity and power that these raised-poor workshops be the place within Re-evaluation Counseling where all people who grew up at or near the bottom of the economic scale come together and reach for closeness with one another. I am particularly pleased that of the seventy-five of us here, more than one-third of us are people of color.

Historically, black labor, white labor, Chinese labor, Japanese labor, European labor, Hispanic labor, Native American labor, etc., as well as male and female labor were all systematically divided from one another by legislation, by differences in rewards offered to each group, and by strike-breaking efforts. It did not take many poor people's rebellions in the early days of the U.S. for the wealthiest owners to recognize that they were vastly outnumbered and would never be able to hold on to their control of the wealth if groups at the bottom were able to effectively join forces against them. They began to reward groups differently and create legislation that set up different levels of poor people and a diffusion of the political power. Doing this would have been impossible if the inherent unity of the people at the bottom of the economic ladder had not been obscured.

One of the primary tasks ahead of us, if we are going to shift things so that every new baby and every young person gets the love, respect, information, medical and educational care, aware attention, and material resources she or he needs to grow up well, is to establish a sense of unity among all poor and working-class people, no matter what their race, sex, religion, or national origin. We must discharge the internalized oppression that sets us against one another. Ultimately, of course, to have the kind of world we want, a world where humans no longer hurt humans, we must establish a sense of deep loving human connection with all people from all class backgrounds. For us to have that kind of world, we will need to do a lot of discharging of our internalized classism and assist people from other classes to discharge theirs. Our leadership in this effort both within and outside of RC is essential.

Although classism has confused all of us from all classes, it seems to me that one advantage we've had is that it is easier to see injustice and correctness from the perspective of the bottom up. We have always known that things are very wrong and must be changed. Now we must learn, starting with our own lives, to take full responsibility for setting things right.

WHAT HAPPENED TO US

In short, what happened to us is that we were told that we are small and worthless. In fact, we are big and valuable. As babies, we looked up at eyes that weren't fully there. As much as they may have loved us, our people were worried or saddened or preoccupied from the oppression they had encountered, and we internalized this lack of confidence, awareness, and joy as our fault. We tried to get them back into awareness with us and couldn't and we felt deeply grieved and ashamed of our failure. Some part of us gave up and went away. No one explained the larger societal picture to us until we had already concluded that we were at fault and insufficient.

In the first year of life most poor babies hear many times as they begin to crawl and explore things, "Stop that." "You are bad." "Don't be so stupid." "You can't have that."As we go out into our neighborhoods we hear similar messages over and over from peers and from other adults. And we are often physically and sometimes sexually abused. These abuses can wipe the confidence out of a child really fast.

We have by age six internalized a huge dose of classism. This sets us up to believe what the schools tell us about our worth. (And now, although it is no one's fault, unaware classism and racism still come at us in our RC Communities, as well.)

RACISM GROWS OUT OF CLASSISM

Classism, once internalized, makes us give up on our own thinking. And racism is classism in its most vicious form. People in the U.S. do not want to admit that racism could be so bad an oppression that it could have the effect of depressing black children's IQ scores, but it is that bad. Hurts from classism have temporarily covered a good bit of the magnificent, flexible intelligence of almost all of us who grew up poor or working-class.

EXPERIENCES WITH LEARNING

The years between birth and two are key years for the learning of language. In fact, whether a child will be an excellent student or an average (or below) student can be predicted fairly accurately at two years of age, just by looking at his or her language skills. And a child's language skills directly reflect the language used in the home. Most poor children never have the opportunity, in the early years, to learn the language system and social behaviors that they will need in order to succeed in our middle-class-oriented school system.

The schools soon give us lots of opportunities to experience failure, and we conclude that we just aren't intelligent enough to compete. We are insulted and humiliated for the way we speak, the way we dress, for what we think, and for what we want. Of course, under such conditions, we don't usually stay very confident, playful, and fun-loving. All too often we completely give up and conclude that we are simply not smart enough to compete successfully. We become cautious and outraged at best and completely discouraged and hopeless at worst. I'm outraged about what the school systems are doing to our poor children (one child in four) right now. It's a disaster. As the ad says, "A mind is a terrible thing to waste."

SOME SUCCEED IN SCHOOL BUT STILL FEEL INFERIOR

Many poor people, including some poor Jews and Asians who have had good language learning opportunities in their early home environments, escaped with enough sense of their intelligence to succeed in school. Although I had as a young child a pump and an outhouse, cold winters, violence, food and clothing shortages, and a sense of impending crisis in my home, I had neighbors who brought in food, parents who adored me, and the good fortune to have been read to.

A neighbor read to me enough to create an interest in books and a sense that the spoken word can be written down. It made, I believe, a great difference between what happened to me in school and what happened to my sister and my cousins and to so many poor children. When I got to school, although my grammar was considered all wrong, and I internalized huge pieces of distress about my thinking and speaking because of efforts to change me, I at least had enough vocabulary and sense of the middle-class language to be able to get good grades. But, although I succeeded, I still thought of myself as "less than." I still struggle with this feeling of inferiority. I have to push myself over all kinds of terror to take up-front leadership like this. (Although, I must say, the terror is discharging fast these days.)

I know that many of you did well in school, but that doesn't mean that you didn't lose a sense that you were smart enough to make things right. Virtually every child who grows up poor, even if they succeed in school, loses a lot of their confidence in their own intelligence. Even if you didn't lose your confidence in the schools, you lost some of it in your homes. It is very hard to feel smart and confident when you grow up in a family that is struggling so hard to survive economically. Way too much is going wrong that a child cannot figure out how to fix. Any child would feel small and stupid in some way in the face of it all.

CLASSISM PERVASIVE

Classism is so pervasive in our society that almost no one can see outside of it. In the U.S. we have a nation full of people who believe that poor people are poor because they are either stupid or lazy. They simply do not see what the oppressive attitudes and lack of opportunity do to a young mind. The consciousness of at least some of the population has been raised somewhat in the last twenty years about racism and sexism. We have a very long way to go, but at least racist and sexist humor are more often interrupted and seen as oppression now.

Almost no one interrupts jokes about workers or poor people who are stupid or lazy, or jokes that are supposed to be funny because they involve "poor" grammar. We still assume most classist attitudes and beliefs are the reality. We roll out the red carpet for those who have money—and offer inferior medical, judicial, and educational opportunities to children born into poverty. We grow up with violence and failure all around us, and although we may not like it, we live with it because we believe what we were taught; that we live in a land of equal opportunity for all, a land where even Abraham Lincoln could become the president.

We are given a woefully incomplete picture of the current reality and of history, and ultimately every poor person internalizes the blame for his or her own situation. We go around thinking, "I must be inferior. If I were just smarter or more hard-working, I, too, would have made it." And, of course, wealthier children internalize the message, "I must deserve this wealth and power. Things are just fine with me. I'm smarter and more responsible than they are." They are taught to see the effects of the oppression that they see on us as reason to continue the oppression. At best they are taught to make things different for us by patronizingly helping us learn to change our ways, with no real sense of the larger societal change or the change in themselves that must take place to end the self-contempt that everyone from every class feels. History is full of this attitude: whole continents have been subjugated by this distress recording.

CLASSIST ATTITUDES CLING TO COUNSELORS

In counseling you can usually feel it coming at you in the form of people assuming in any interaction that they are counselor and you are the client. The people underneath this distress are deeply good, but their patterns make them assume that you need help more than they do. And they certainly don't see that you could be of help to them. They are brought up with so much isolation that they just don't notice that we have something intact that they could use. They don't notice that we know something about generosity and closeness that they just don't understand (to the extent that they carry the pattern, that is—not every middle- or owning-class person carries the pattern). Nobody ever treated them in such a way that they *could* know it. The way our intelligence works here is incomprehensible to a middle-class or owning-class pattern. And since they don't notice, and we assume they know better, we have come to de-value this thing we know.

We are bewildered by their selfishness and lack of interest in us, but we assume that their model of leadership is what we should aspire to. Since we don't have the pseudo-confidence, the polished, smooth way of speaking and operating, we let them lead in any interaction or any group. We assume that they are smarter and better leaders, we give them dominance, and we secretly resent them for taking it. We are put off by any traces of officiousness and love of the limelight, but we endure them rather than risk ourselves failing as leaders. We just won't risk one more humiliation. And even if we did succeed, we fear that we might lose all the people who love us, our people. So we stay subordinate in every way, except way down deep where we still dream about how things could be. That's one thing we can always count on. There is a deeper, more beautiful vision within all of us, from every class, a longing for things to be right for everyone.

The different levels of classist patterns form a perfect hook with one another: inferiority hooks superiority; superiority hooks inferiority. If anyone from either side completely gives up his or her pattern, the other side of the hook has to shift. We need to discharge and choose, discharge and choose until we can stay with ourselves, stay thinking and bold in the face of all patterns of domination and pretense. *Their* patterns are held in place by self-invalidation (I'm guilty and bad), and terror; *ours* are held in place by self-invalidation (I'm worthless, stupid), and terror.

Each side wears their terror in different ways, but the fact is that the current situation is invalidating and terrifying to every little boy and girl growing up in this society today. The current situation is bad for all children. All of us want things to change, but we're terrified of the consequences of stepping out of our side of the pattern first. We all need to come to love the feeling of taking correct action and feeling terrified. This time we can discharge our terror.

WE NEED TO KNOW OUR REAL HISTORY

We have been stuck in this interlocking of dominance-subordination confusions for a long time. I will spend a little bit of time here talking about our history because to know our history is to begin taking the shame and blame off of ourselves and putting it on the larger society, where it belongs. A good book for you to read to get a picture of what has happened in this country to poor people is *A*

People's History of the U.S. by Howard Zinn. (Editor's note: *A People's History of England* by A.L. Morton is excellent for readers in Britain.) The reality that we need to hold up to everyone is that no poor person is to blame for her oppression. How wealth is distributed, how much of it stays in the hands of the wealthy and how much of it gets into the hands of the other groups, is directly the result of decisions made by our legislators. And since the earliest times in this country, the wealthiest people have been the ones holding most of the decision-making power. In the 1700s, ninety percent of the population was excluded from office because they were not landholders. The pattern has continued until today, when most of the campaign contributions come from the wealthy and thus determine to a large extent the decisions of legislators. Until there is a limit to campaign spending, most elected officials must cater to the interests of those who can pay for their exorbitant campaign expenditures. They continue to make decisions that serve the economic interests of the wealthy.

GREATER WEALTH AND GREATER POVERTY

Most recently we have seen that the economic decisions made by legislators during the 1980s have had the effect of redistributing wealth in the direction of the very wealthiest people. The top 1% enjoyed a windfall. The next 19% did somewhat less well. The bottom 80% were left significantly worse off. In a recent study of taxation, it was determined that the wealthiest people pay 7% of their income in taxes. The middle-income people pay 10%, and the lowest-income people pay 13.7%. We are beginning to see the effects of this in society now. As the economic situation gets worse, we're sure to see more scapegoating of people of color, as well as Jews and Gay people.

Wealthy adults apparently have forgotten, because of their oppression, that their real interests are precisely the same as our real interests. Our child poverty rate rose over the last period of time from 1-in-7 to 1-in-5 to 1-in-4 preschool children. Every 35 seconds, one new baby is born into poverty. Every 14 minutes an infant dies during the first year of life. Tonight 100,000 children will be homeless. In the last census more than 1.5 million mothers reported that they leave their infants and preschoolers home alone unattended while they work because they don't have money to afford housing, food, and childcare. During the last ten years, services to children were cut by 50%, homicide became the leading cause of death among black males, school dropout rates rose as high as 30% in some cities, and our prison population doubled. We have a higher percent of our population living in prison than does any other country in the world. Our prisons, our "mental health" system, and now our streets are becoming overcrowded with poor people whose sense of hope for a decent future has been crushed by a world that offered them far more harshness than they could bear as children.

POLITICAL POWER DIFFUSED

Why haven't we changed this situation? Because our political power to change things has been diffused since the late 1700s, when racial issues were first systematically used to pull poor people apart. In those early days the condition of poor whites in servitude was not much better than the conditions of slaves. Masters could make about $250 a year from slaves or servants and keep them for about $12. Servants were beaten, whipped, raped, humiliated, and overworked. They couldn't marry without their master's consent. Those who didn't die paying off the seven years of servitude they owed for their passage to this country were most often left hopeless, broken, and in debt to their masters and could never change their conditions of life.

At the same point in history there were Native American hostilities and slave revolts beginning. By 1750 in the Carolinas there were 25,000 whites, 90% of them poor and excluded from office, and there were 40,000 black slaves. Racism was not yet installed on poor white people. They worked with blacks in the fields and in the kitchens, and they intermarried at high rates. They had as yet not learned to look upon black people as inferior. The court records are full of documents of intermarriage.

As time went on and the number of rebellions grew, the wealthy landowners began to recognize that, given that they were so greatly outnumbered, even though they had the militia on their side they must pass laws that interfered with the organization of outraged Native Americans, whites, and blacks. They actively began to spread racist attitudes to poor whites and passed laws forbidding intermarriage. They also gave poor whites small economic advantages over blacks and made treaties with Native Americans contingent upon the return of runaway slaves. Poor white people soon took on the oppressor role. When people lack confidence, they can easily be led to take on oppressive attitudes toward others. That's why wealthy children take on classism and racism, and that is why poor people took on racism.

Over time, the outraged poor groups lost a sense of their natural alliance against the control of wealth and decision-making by the wealthy. They began to see one another as the problem, acting out their internalized oppression on each other at every available opportunity. Racism, first attached to Native Americans and black people in this country, soon became attached to Hispanics and Asians. Although various labor groups and some politicians have tried, with varying degrees of success, to organize these diverse groups into one powerful force against classism, the inter-group hostility remains strong and weakens efforts for change. I work near a Chrysler plant and increasingly I see very racist, anti-Japanese bumper stickers. White auto workers now believe that Japanese people, even Japanese-Americans, are their problem.

RACE-BAITING

In elections over the past ten years, politicians who serve the interest of the wealthiest people have fanned the fires of racism that separate groups by campaign ads and speeches that suggest that federal taxes finance the transfer of white income to blacks and other minorities. They would have us believe, too, that federal regulations serve to cut back white control of schools, jobs, and neighborhoods. They hold off pressure to raise taxes on the wealthiest group by showing examples of blacks or Hispanics abusing welfare money. White working-class and middle-class people who feel economically pressured already see people of color as the problem, as they watch these campaign ads. The fact that the great majority of the poor people in this country are white is almost totally obscured in the political rhetoric. The strategy is known as race-baiting, and it has existed in our country since the earliest days. The consequences for poor people have been devastating.

WARS

Last fall we saw an example of another common historical pattern. When class struggles or dissatisfaction with internal injustices get high, patriotism and loyalty to the government can be fanned, diffusing class anger. For instance, wonderful debates about the possibility of increasing taxes on the wealthy were going on in Congress until the Gulf War began. Suddenly all the emphasis was on patriotism and the foreign enemy that we all must fight. A similar diffusion of class outrage and analysis with patriotism occurred with the American Revolution, the Civil War, the Spanish-American War, World Wars I and II, the Korean War (which initiated the Cold War), and the Vietnam War (which ended the War on Poverty).

WE ARE GOOD

We are brilliant, heroic people, no matter how much we may look and feel otherwise. It took massive amounts of oppressive legislation over a long and difficult history to lead us to this point of discouragement. We've done well considering the situation. We are not, not one of us, to blame for having such a hard time making our lives go well. We have, each one of us, fought as hard as we could to hold on to our belief in ourselves and one another and to operate over the terror.

In spite of all the oppression that has come our way, in spite of all the messages that we are inferior, we have kept many areas of clarity. For instance, our lack of pretense makes us very likeable. People can see who we are; we're real and available in most interactions. We know how to survive under difficult conditions. We have a keen understanding and compassion for the oppressed. We can be fully *for* people. We are, as a group, extremely generous people. And generosity *is* intelligence. It is the intelligence the world needs. Recently I was delighted to read documentation of our generosity. A study of contributions to charitable causes showed contribution levels are the highest by percent of income contributed in the lowest-income neighborhoods and go down from there as the income of the neighborhood rises. We are good, straight-forward people. Although we have been systematically divided, we still understand, I believe, "All for one and one for all" better than any other group.

Middle-class and owning-class people are deeply good too, and they want us. Their patterns are paper tigers, just feelings of inferiority in disguise. The more dominant and intimidating they look, the more scared they are. It doesn't help to be hard on them, as much as you might feel like being that way. We just have to discharge that outrage. They are lonely, scared, little boys and girls inside, dying for someone to notice and think well about them, just as we are. Anyone from any oppressor group can only change when they can focus on their real goodness. We will only be effective in changing their attitudes and in reclaiming our own power when we give up blaming them or playing the inferior side in any interaction.

The enemy is classism, not middle- or owning-class people. The same lesson that we learned about men and sexism applies here. Everybody has been terribly victimized by class oppression. We know now that money and more wealth is not what wealthier people really want. We can't let them run things when they are still confused about using people for their own gains. That pattern must be stopped. It doesn't help anyone. They are longing for aware attention, for people who can love them, accept them, and help them discharge their aloneness, so that they can once again sense that wonderful feeling of connection with all people.

STEP OUTSIDE VICTIMIZATION

So let us get smart about our patterns and theirs. We'll do some demonstrations later on to practice confident and loving interruption of classism and pretense. We don't have to be at the bottom ever again, in any human interaction. We can give up wearing "poor" patterns and all that that means for us.

We must discharge our feelings of insignificance, worthlessness, shame, hopelessness, guilt, fear, stupidity, and anger, not continue to act on them. We can stand eye to eye with people and give up inferiority and powerlessness. We can assume that we can get the lives we want for ourselves, and we can take every action step necessary to make our dreams become a reality.

Until we have discharged all the internalized classism, to get the lives we want we will have to exercise very srict discipline over the feelings this brutal oppression has left us with. Depending on how each of us has internalized classism, that will mean such things as: keeping our commitments to ourselves and to one another (i.e., doing what we say we are going to do, showing up when we say we are going to show up), figuring out how to get enough financial resource in our lives so that crises are not a way of life and worries about money don't take up our attention, setting about learning the skills and getting the information we need to do what we want to do, reaching for the best and most supportive relationships we can build, fighting for what we want while assuming that people want to be our allies (discharging the fear and anger, not bringing them into our present-time battles), and making our own re-emergence a priority.

We can, by respecting each other well and counseling each other well right here, tackle that vicious irrationality, so little understood in our world, called classism. We understand the closeness work that we must do, the coming back to one another that must happen so that we can feel deeply connected and thus deeply powerful. We know now that we are all one people. We will be able to feel it more and more as we discharge our isolation.

Our real interests are exactly and precisely the same as those of all other poor people and of middle- and owning-class people, too. They have always been the same. We have much to learn from the other classes, and they have much to learn from us. We get to set high goals, go all out to create the lives we want for ourselves, and refuse to settle. Everyone will benefit when we take such strong steps outside of our victimization. We get to control our own state of mind. Our sense of worth need not be dependent on their approval of us.

WE HAVE A SOLUTION TO CLASSISM

We have the solution. Right now, at this workshop, we have a chance to shift history. Harriet Tubman went back to free hundreds of her people from the chains of slavery. We can go back and get the invisible chains of classism off one another right here.

Fortunately, our past does not equal our future. We can discharge through all the early failures and disappointments that keep our lives from being all that we've ever dreamed of and more. We can create the future we want for ourselves and for our people. We can decide to no longer be victim of the false messages of our class background.

As we go about trying to build a powerful poor and working-class people's movement, we must eliminate racism and work for peace. Sexism also must be addressed. Two out of every three poor adults in this country are women. Family work both in and out of RC is essential, because the oppression of the larger society is internalized and is first passed on to our children within our own homes.

It is difficult for all of us to think of ourselves as world changers. We were all brutally socialized into thinking of ourselves as incompetent to get even our own lives in order. We grew up feeling alone and powerless in our struggle to make things right for ourselves and our people. The feeling is chronic, and we cannot see out of it. We may get a glimmer now and then, but we quickly forget and settle into our more familiar sense of insignificance. Fortunately, chronics are just well-practiced feelings that easily give way to discharge.

This process works. Just by using it well we will get our own lives in better order than we ever hoped for, and have lots of attention and time left over to influence ever wider circles of the world. Therefore, we might as well begin right now. Let's take ourselves seriously as world changers and recognize that we do hold history in our hands. There is a high and significant destiny for all of us who persist in using this process well. Our timidity will discharge, leaving behind a sense of boldness and ease of functioning that will attract large numbers of people to us. And they will want us to teach them what we know about reclaiming intelligence and power.

We do have the solution to human irrationality. Everyone has been looking for it since time immemorial. Think of it. It is so simple: human irrationality happens just because distress recordings obscure thinking. And we know how to discharge distress recordings, clearing the way for our magnificent brains to function rationally. Brilliance is just the absence of distress recordings in action.

Think how privileged you are to be among the fortunate few who currently know how to reclaim your intelligence through discharge. You did hit the lottery! Think of the impact you can have, knowing what you know. Do not let your chronic hopelessness interfere with going to classes every week and getting regular sessions. This process, that as yet so few people in the world know how to use, is the solution to that irrationality we call classism. If we share it with others, the isolation will discharge, leaving people deeply connected and classism will be eliminated.

BUILDING RAISED-POOR AND PEOPLE-OF-COLOR COMMUNITIES

Although my impatience usually leaves me feeling like things are going much too slowly in my Region (Brandywine), it is clear even to me that we have had successes in growing raised-poor and black RC leadership. Some of you have asked how we've done it. I'm not sure of all the dynamics that have worked. I always seem to be clearer about the mistakes I've made.

One thing I know that I've done that has been important is that I haven't tried to bring one or two poor or black people into a huge white middle-class workshop or even into a class. I started most of the black people in classes in which they were dominant in terms of number, with maybe just one other, carefully chosen, white person besides myself. Or I put two or three promising people of color right into my leadership class. And when I had three black people ready to go to an overnight workshop, I made the workshop be just for six people (three black people and three very real and present white people).

I only started bringing raised-poor and black people to large Regional workshops when I knew they would have a number of people like themselves there, when they had regular Co-Counselors, when they loved the process, and when they had already made some strong, supportive relationships with white people in the Community. And then I was very clear with the white Community about how they were to act around these people. I told them that they were first to remember that they were absolutely good and, second, to refrain from counseling on anything about black people with black people. If they needed to counsel about the issue of race, take it to a white counselor.

To help pay for workshops, we charge everybody in the Community who can pay, a dollar extra per night of class. Nobody has objected yet. I also used a bit extra of the upfront counseling time doing demonstrations with the raised-poor and black people so that others could see them as people and see how they might be loved and counseled well. That also made it clear to people that I was going to make the development of poor, working-class, and people-of-color leaders a Community priority for the next period of time.

Most of all, I just recruited well. I went after people who already had good people-skills and a lot of aware attention. They came into the Community and were sought after right from the start. Now we have two black teachers, and Lillian Jones is an Area Reference Person.

The real key to keeping people of color in RC is simple: Just look into their eyes and hearts and love them for the human beings they are, like you would with anyone else. Whites have to give up being gooey, patronizing, and over-solicitous. That is a kind of neediness and it puts people in a position to have to take care of your feelings by acting appreciative and affirming of you, whether they feel like it right then or not. Just be as real as you possibly can be, like yourself a lot, and be an equal and, before you know it, you will find that your new Co-Counselor will contradict your isolation in amazing ways.

WHAT PEOPLE OF COLOR KNOW

To do this work well, you need to remember that you are blameless, but also understand that people of color understand some things that most of us white people don't get yet. For centuries, white people overlooked what Native Americans know. For instance, Native Americans have always had clarity about caring for the earth. White people just didn't notice the intelligence that was intact in Native people about this issue. Now, finally, as we begin to reach a crisis point for the earth and air around us, our consciousness is beginning to be raised.

Another example of something people of color know was illustrated in the movie, "Glory." There was a scene where the black men got together the night before the long-prepared-for and dreaded battle. The support and encouragement they gave each other was so real and beautiful. It was different in tone from what you'd see happening between white people. Not that white people don't support each other well, but there was something different, something very similar to what black people have brought to my Region. Sometimes you can feel it in black churches or at funerals. I want to learn more about whatever this quality is: I want to have that kind of love and support more and more a part of my life.

I read recently that studies show that Japanese mothers spend twice as much time holding their babies as do American mothers. They usually sleep with them also. And the Hispanic mothers I've worked with have a sense of community about each other's children. They all watch out for all the young people. They have an attitude of, "Their children are my children." These are just a few small examples of intelligence in action that whites don't notice. When our hurts still interfere with our own flexible intelligence, we just can't see or understand these ways that the minds of many people of color are clear.

Asians, Hispanics, Native Americans, blacks and other people of color have never internalized the distress called "white." I think "white" is a more encompassing, broader distress than "white racism," but probably led to the susceptibility to "white racism." I think there was something terrifying that happened throughout Europe for centuries, something that had to do with warrior states, dominance, and the heavily exaggerated class structure. We have our roots in a very brutal way of life for little boys and girls. We are doing great overtop of it.

We need to take pride in our goodness, but it is very clear to me that people of color have areas of clarity that most of us still can't notice and that they will bring to us. I watch people of color in all-white groups and they often just seem to be at a loss with our stiffness and isolation from one another. It is confusing to them. I heard one Native American woman in counseling ask incredulously, "What happened to you white people anyway?" I don't know, but I think early separation and the harshness of thousands of years of conquest is at the heart of it.

RAISED-POOR COMMITMENT

People have asked me to talk about a Raised-Poor Commitment. I'd like to hold off on finalizing a commitment until we do more work with raised-poor people. One that I sometimes use is—

> "I am a bold and brilliant thinker. I can change the world. I refuse to settle for anything less than complete liberation of my mind and the minds of all people from the effects of classism. I will expect and reach for complete respect, complete equality, and complete closeness, and I will take complete responsibility for seeing that all human beings get treated well."

(Usually, I just use the third sentence, because commitments work best for me if they are short. I like it because it is a commitment to use the discharge process, as well as to act outside of the distress in other ways.)

Another commitment is:

> "I solemnly promise to always remember it was never my/our fault that I/we was/were born into a society which uses poverty to perpetuate the oppression of all people. We are the majority and the natural leaders of the entire world. I promise to remember my/our goodness, strength, and intelligence. I will settle for nothing less than complete respect and complete opportunity for everyone. Furthermore, I will personally see to it!"

Try things out, see what works for you, and share it with me. But don't get so focused on commitments that you forget that discharging the early hopelessness and reaching out for closeness in the present has to happen. Tell your early life stories over and over again. Spend some time in sessions exploring what was good about your background, too. As counselors, remember that most raised-poor people don't discharge well when you tease them or point out their pattern in any way. We just feel too bad about our shortcomings to be able to discharge when too much of our attention is directed toward them. The contradiction comes from being able to relaxedly look past the patterns and see the dignity of the human being that has survived.

The counselor can't come in as the "fixer." The counselor has to be fully for you, fully with you, fully respectful of your dignity, as you go after the distress. Counselors also need to remind us to take pride in our successes and set goals so that we remember that we get to create the life we want for ourselves, not just take what comes. We need to be coaches for one another—"You can do it! You can do it!" Wherever and however you can get the heaviest discharge, as long as you are not being oppressive to your counselor, go for it.

CONCLUSION

We are brilliant, each and every one of us. When we have appeared dull, ineffectual, or stupid, it was because we were acting within the internalized messages of class oppression. We can fully reclaim our intelligence. Let's discharge our rigidities and become once again fully flexible and effective thinkers. Let's discharge every bit of the terror and outrage we thought we'd have to carry around forever. It's going to be so much easier to live and lead when we do.

Until the distress is discharged, let's steer these minds of ours away from the distress by asking ourselves the right questions. Let's let our minds mull over questions that are empowering rather than self-defeating. Rather than, "Can I do it?", ask, "What do I need to do to make this work?" Rather than, "Am I lovable?", ask, "Who loves me, and who do I love?" Rather than, "Oh no, do I have to face this day?", ask, "What's great about being alive today?" Rather than, "Can I lead?", ask, "What shall I lead next to build up my confidence in myself as a leader?" Successful action steps will build our confidence. We must act.

We are born to be leaders. Our process will take us there if we use it systematically. Our individual and collective leadership is needed to set things right, both within and outside of RC. Let us begin our movement here with one another. Let us create unity. Let's play and have fun together between sessions and be as present and real with each other as we possibly can as counselors. Let's get "Free at last!" Poverty is completely unnecessary. Patterns of dominance and subordination will discharge. When we give up inferiority and regain our flexible thinking, we will find the elegant solution for our own life and for society as a whole.

When large numbers of people are using this process regularly to overcome their hopelessness and to restore their joy, confidence, and good thinking, we will have the society we all long for, a society unlike any in history with an economy that works for all people.

Someday we *will* have a world full of stable, strong families, where all children get what they need to grow up well. Can you imagine it? Beautiful countrysides; safe, clean streets; friendly, happy people everywhere; and children playing together in thoughtful, validating ways because they've gotten so much aware attention that they just feel good. It is possible. It is possible to bring up a world full of children who think clearly about one another and about the earth and air around us. We do know what to do now. We know what children need and we know what poor people need. This process is a breakthrough in history. So much is in bud here.

As Tracy Chapman has said so beautifully, "Poor people are gonna rise up. Can you hear it? It sounds like a whisper."